Click, Connect, Compute

DATA, BIG AND SMALL

Author: Dr Dharini Balasubramaniam • Illustrator: Luke Séguin-Magee

WAYLAND

MIX
Paper | Supporting
responsible forestry
FSC® C104740
FSC
www.fsc.org

DATA USE TERMS
AND CONDITIONS

CONTENTS

What *are* data?

Data form the basis of so much of what we do in computer science. The software programs written by computer scientists typically work with data to solve problems. Let's explore what 'data' means, first of all.

Datum and data

A *datum* is a single piece of fact or detail about something. The plural form of datum is data, which is commonly used.

In computer science, the word 'data' refers to facts, measurements or other details about something that can help us to solve problems or complete some work. Data need to be collected and stored so that they can be used when they are needed. 

Examples of data

Data are produced in large amounts every second of every day.

Astronomers use automatic telescopes to watch the sky and record what is seen.

Businesses record what people buy online or in shops.

Schools record the work done by pupils and the marks teachers give them.

The life of data

Like people, data can go through many stages of life. These include:

1. **Creation:** how data come into being.

2. **Storage:** how data are kept to be used later.

3. **Sharing and use:** how data are shared between different. computer systems and used.

4. **Archiving:** how data that are not regularly used are kept for records.

5. **Deletion:** how data that are no longer needed are erased.

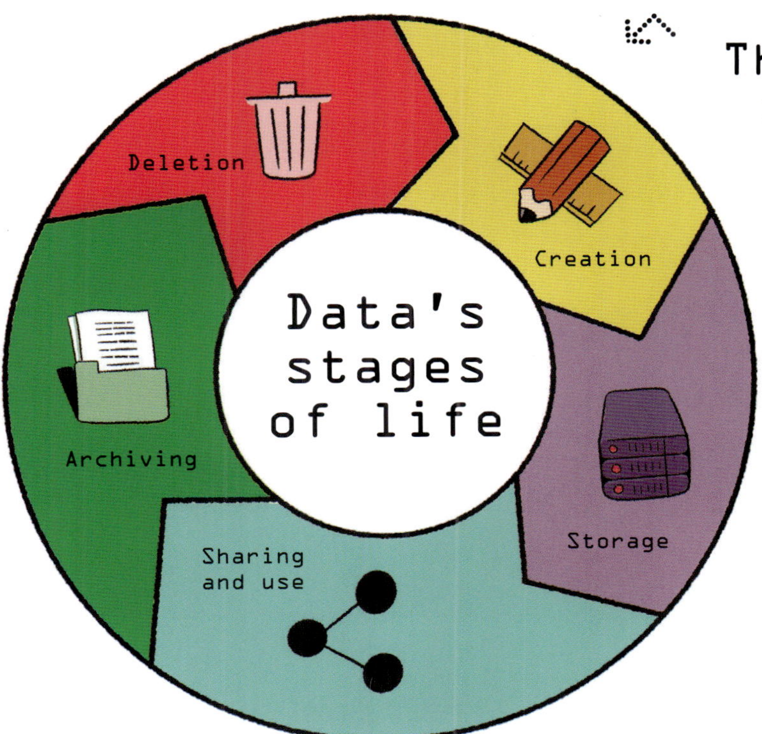

Data, information and knowledge

Data begin to have meaning and value for us when we start to interact with them.

Data

Data are 'raw' facts and numbers in the form they are collected without any work done on them. They don't have a lot of meaning in that raw form.

These numbers don't mean much as a list of raw data.

33:42, 32:40, 32:05, 30:22, 29:07, 28:40, 28:33, 27:58, 27:52, 27:36, 26:13, 25:45

Information

We get **information** when we process or interpret data to give them meaning. This processing can include thinking about where the data come from, organising or summarising data, and putting them into groups of similar data.

In our example above, we begin to get information from the data when we know that the numbers are the times taken by a runner to complete a 5-km run once a month over 12 months.

We can then also **interpret** the data to get more information: the runner has run faster each month.

Knowledge

Knowledge is the understanding we have of a subject or topic. We can improve our knowledge of a topic by taking in information about that topic (doing research) and having more experiences related to that topic.

So, we think about the information we have about the runner and about the context (circumstances) to add to our knowledge of the whole situation. If the runner keeps training, and eating and resting well, they can keep improving their time until they reach their full potential.

Wisdom

When we talk about knowledge outside of computer science, we sometimes see a pyramid structure with four ideas: data, information, knowledge and wisdom.

Wisdom is thought of as a deeper understanding of *why* things happen, allowing people to use knowledge to make good decisions.

We don't usually associate wisdom with computers, but we can still use it to see how it builds on and relates to the previous three ideas.

Data are vital

People, organisations and computers use data to make decisions. Typically, the more data we have, the better informed our decisions can be.

It's a science!

Working with data is a scientific discipline called **data science**. It uses ideas and techniques from other disciplines, such as statistics and computer science – particularly artificial intelligence (AI) – to discover insights (gain knowledge) from data. This helps with decision-making and future-planning.

Uses of data science

Data science can be used to understand all sorts of situations.

<u>What</u> is happening?

Data science can help us to understand what has happened in the past and is happening at present.

<u>Why</u> is it happening?

Data science can help us to understand why things are happening the way they are.

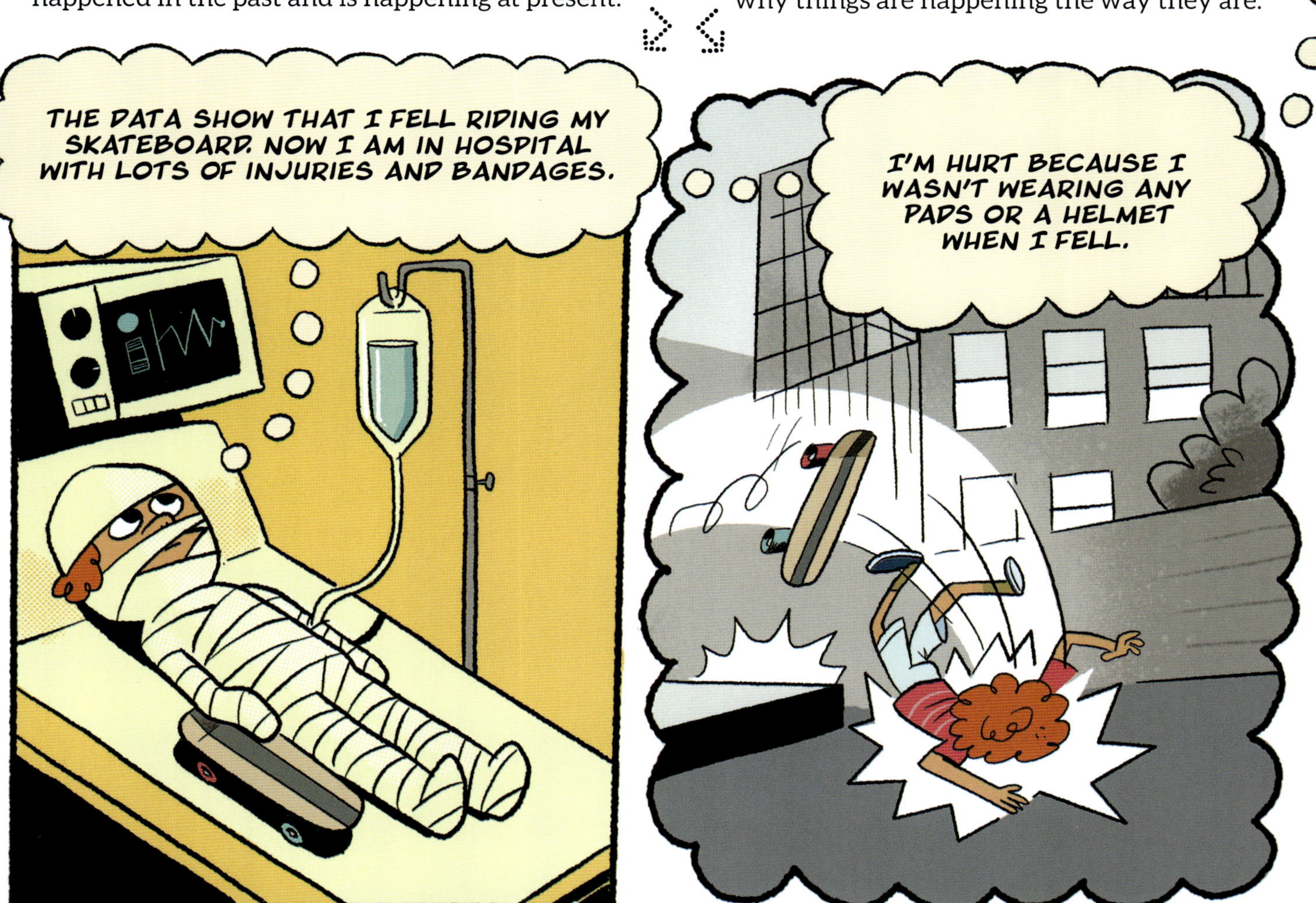

What <u>will</u> happen?

Data science can help us to predict what is likely to happen in the future based on what has happened in the past.

What <u>should</u> happen?

Data science can help us to decide the ideal actions for the future.

Find out about one of the 'fathers of data science' – John Tukey – on page 30.

Find out about a pioneer who uses HUGE amounts of data, 'the godmother of AI' – Fei-Fei Li – on page 29.

Where do data come from?

Before we can work with data ourselves or process them with computer programs, we need to *gather* them. People and organisations use many digital (computer-based) devices, so a lot of data can be collected by and from these devices.

What's your source?

A **data source** is something from which we can get data. There are many data sources in the world, such as when scientists study nature and record what they see.

As we go about our daily lives – studying, working, playing, travelling and shopping – our activities generate a lot of data, which are recorded. Some of our activities are in person and others are done online (using a digital device). In other words, data can be produced in the **physical** and **digital** worlds.

Governments and other organisations collect data directly from people by doing **surveys** (such as a census or an opinion poll). Over time, these become very useful collections of data that organisations can use to decide how best to improve people's lives.

Data sets

A **data set** is a collection of related data – data that are connected to a common topic or activity. Data in a data set can be accessed individually or processed as a collection.

For example, climate scientists may want to look at daily weather readings in a given national park over a whole year. Bringing this information together would form a data set containing weather data for the park.

Scientists can look at the weather readings for the park on a specific day during that year, or look at patterns in weather for the year based on the full data set or, for example, predict the weather a month from now.

Getting the format right

Data are most useful when they can be automatically (and so quickly) processed by computers to solve problems, or to present the information from the data in an easy form for humans to understand.

Data formats

To start with, data need to be structured in specific ways so that they can be processed by computer programs. This structure is known as the **data format.** Depending on what they represent and how they will be used, data can be held in different formats.

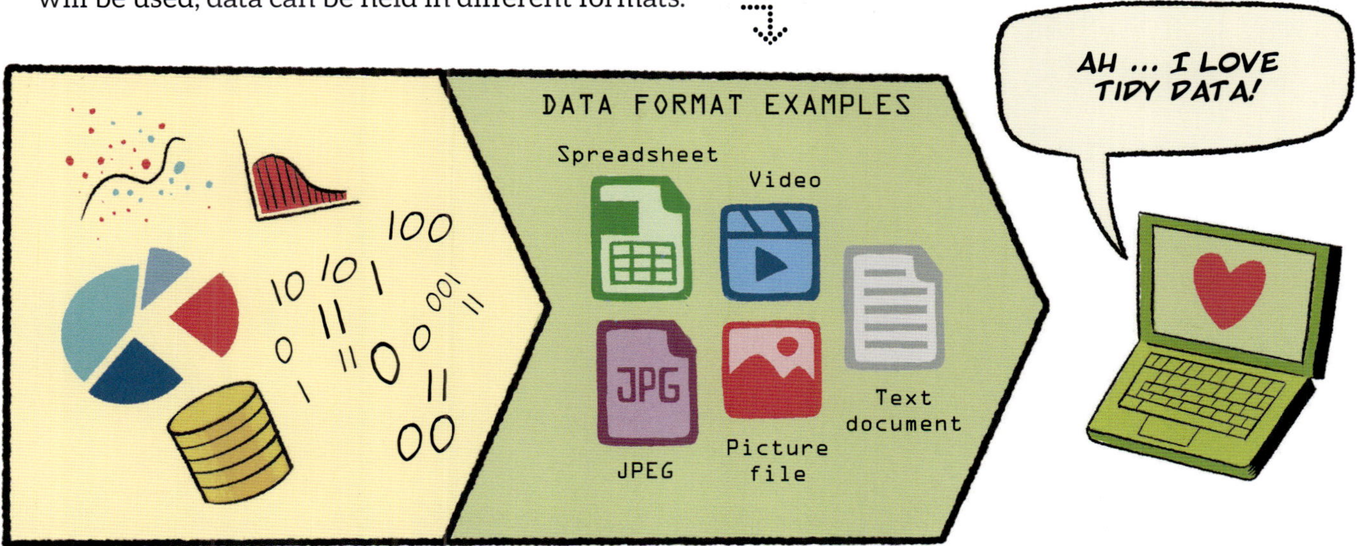

For example, let's say we want to record data about a person.
The name of the person (such as 'Kira') will be in **text** format. Their age will be a **number** (such as 11). Their **picture** will be an image. Each datum represents one detail (e.g. age) about the person in one format (e.g. number).

When we put these details together, we get a more **composite** format that represents the whole person.

Storing all those data

We need to think about how we can keep or
store these data while they are useful,
as well as what we want to do with them.

How long do data live?

Some data are produced and used only while a computer
program is running. When the program finishes, the data are not
needed any more and they disappear. These are called **transient
data**. ('Transient' means temporary or not lasting for long.)

For example, we can enter numbers as data into a calculator
program that helps people with arithmetic. As soon as we
have finished using the program, the numbers will be lost.

Some data are collected or processed while
the program is running and are needed even
after the program has finished. These are kept
to be used later and are called **persistent data**.
('Persistent' means existing for a long time.)

For example, banks will keep 
records for many years of the
money going in and out of
any bank accounts that are
held with them.

Why so long?

How long persistent data live depends on why they are needed. Sometimes they are kept for a few months or years, and sometimes they are kept for as long as possible. For example, scientific observations are usually kept for a long time so people can refer to them for as long as the information may be of interest.

Using computers

Persistent data are kept in a **data store**. Files in computers and databases are examples of data stores. These can be held on personal devices, external devices (e.g. hard drives) or on the cloud, which is a network of computer resources that can be accessed via the Internet.

Data stored within or outside computers have to be accessible so they can be used to complete tasks. We can:

- manually find the data using file management on a computer (e.g. folders)
- use cloud access programs provided by service companies (e.g. Google or Apple)
- use programs written by computer scientists that will access and use the data automatically.

Find out about database pioneer – Edgar F. Codd – on page 28.

The value is in the processing

Data have to be processed to get useful information from them. Processing can include all sorts of activities.

Example: pets at home

Imagine you want to find out more about what kinds of pet your class have at home. We can do this by asking each pupil to answer questions on the class computer.

The first question is about the type of pet (for example, cat, dog, parrot, chicken, gerbil, rabbit, lizard, snake, etc.). The second question is about the main colour of the pet (for example, brown, grey, red, or green).

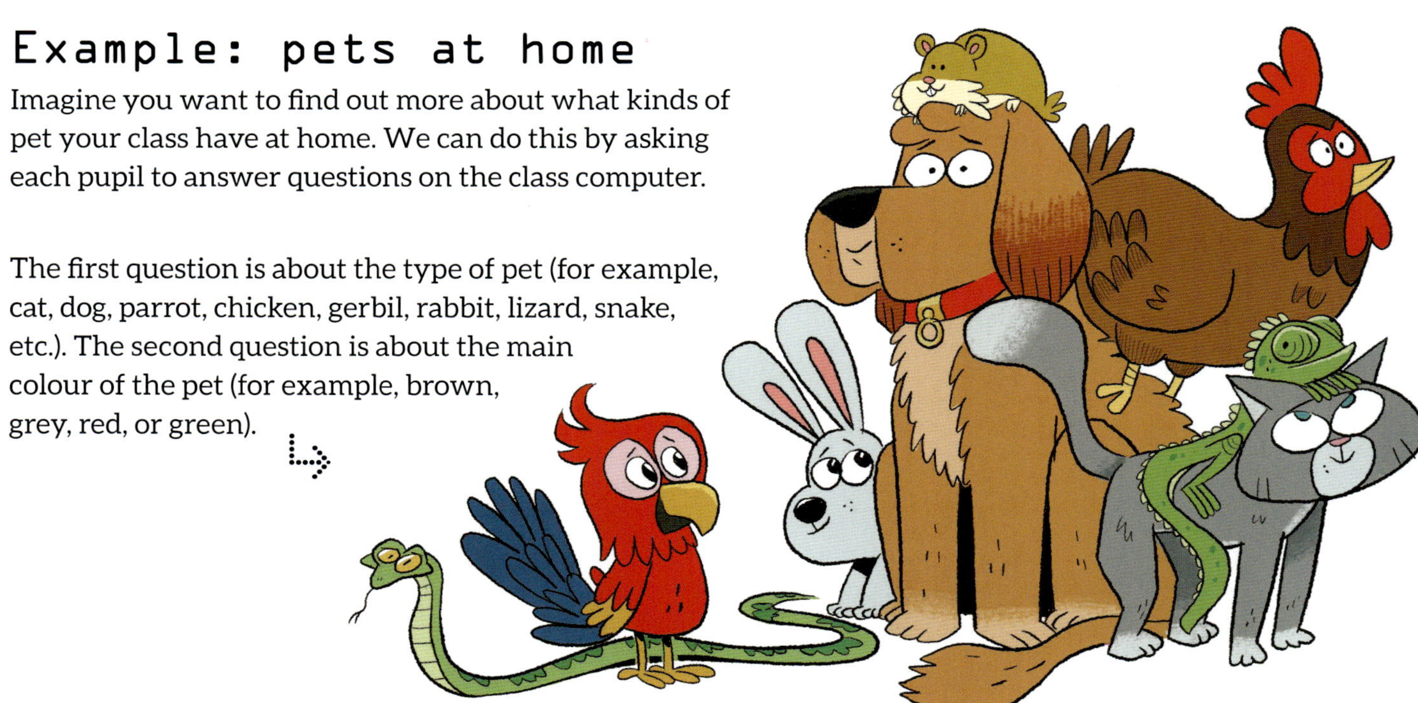

Processes for processing

Validation is the process of checking that the data are correct, in the right format (see page 13) and all relevant to our task. Accurate and relevant data are essential for people and programs to make correct decisions.

So, in our example of pets at home, a computer program could make sure that answers to the first question are all typical pet animals (so, for example, we can't have a lion or a water bottle!) and that answers to the second question are all colours.

```
DOG
Can be a pet?: Yes
What colour?: BROWN

LIZARD
Can be a pet?: Yes
What colour?: GREEN
```

Classification is the process of grouping the data into categories that share common features.

So, our pet program could group pets into categories such as birds, mammals and reptiles.

Analysis is the process of discovering useful information from the data for making decisions or solving problems.

Here, the pet program would seek to find the most common colour among pets in the class.

Reporting is the process of presenting the data in an easy-to-understand form.
So, we could have our program produce graphs that show the findings of the analysis.

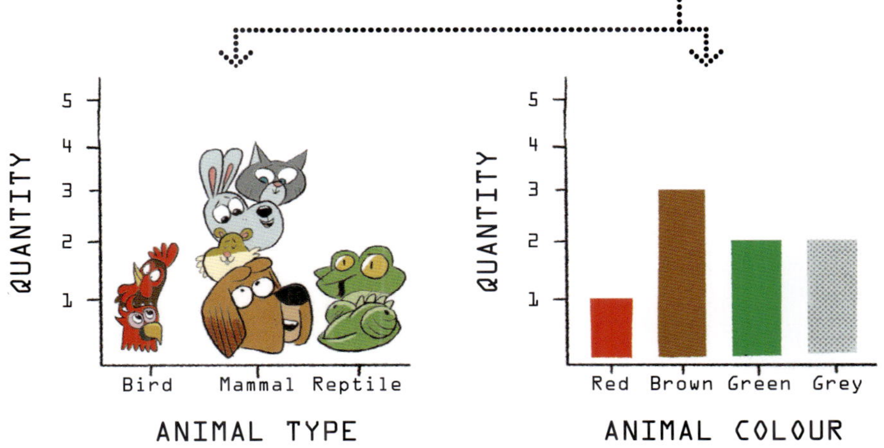

Find out about information and search engine pioneer – Karen Spärck Jones – on page 30.

Picture it!

Data can be presented or reported in different ways. While computers can process large amounts of numbers and text very quickly, humans usually find it easier to make sense of data shown in visual forms. It is also easier for humans to spot patterns in visual data.

How do we picture data?

There are different ways of visualising or picturing data. Let's look at some examples.

Different ways of visualising data suit different purposes, so we have to think carefully before choosing a visualisation.

For example, **trees** are good for showing connections and structure at different levels. ....

Maps are useful for showing patterns and distributions. ....

Find out about information visualisation pioneer – Ben Shneiderman – on page 29.

Word clouds

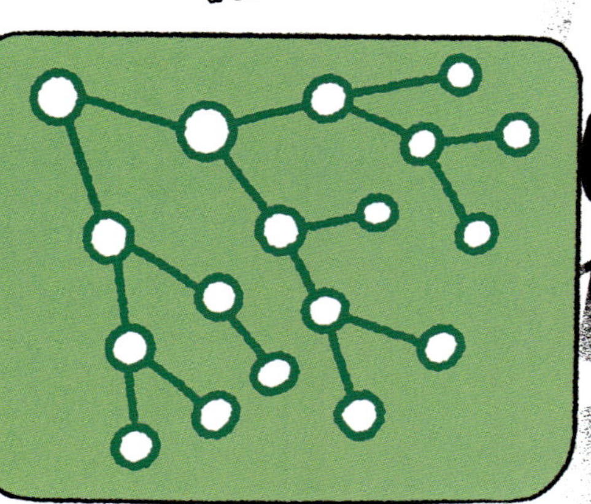

Trees

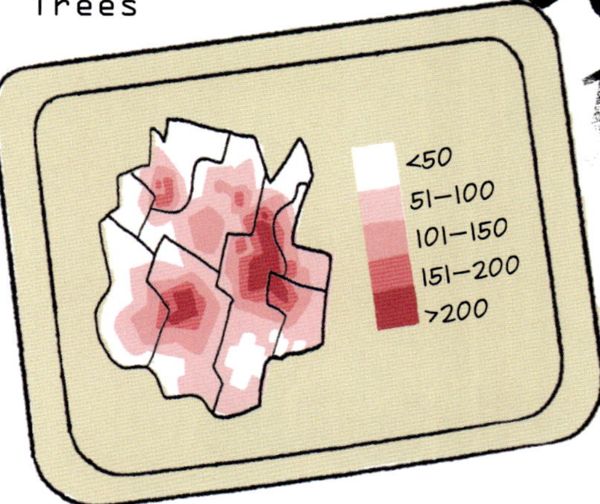

Maps

Tables

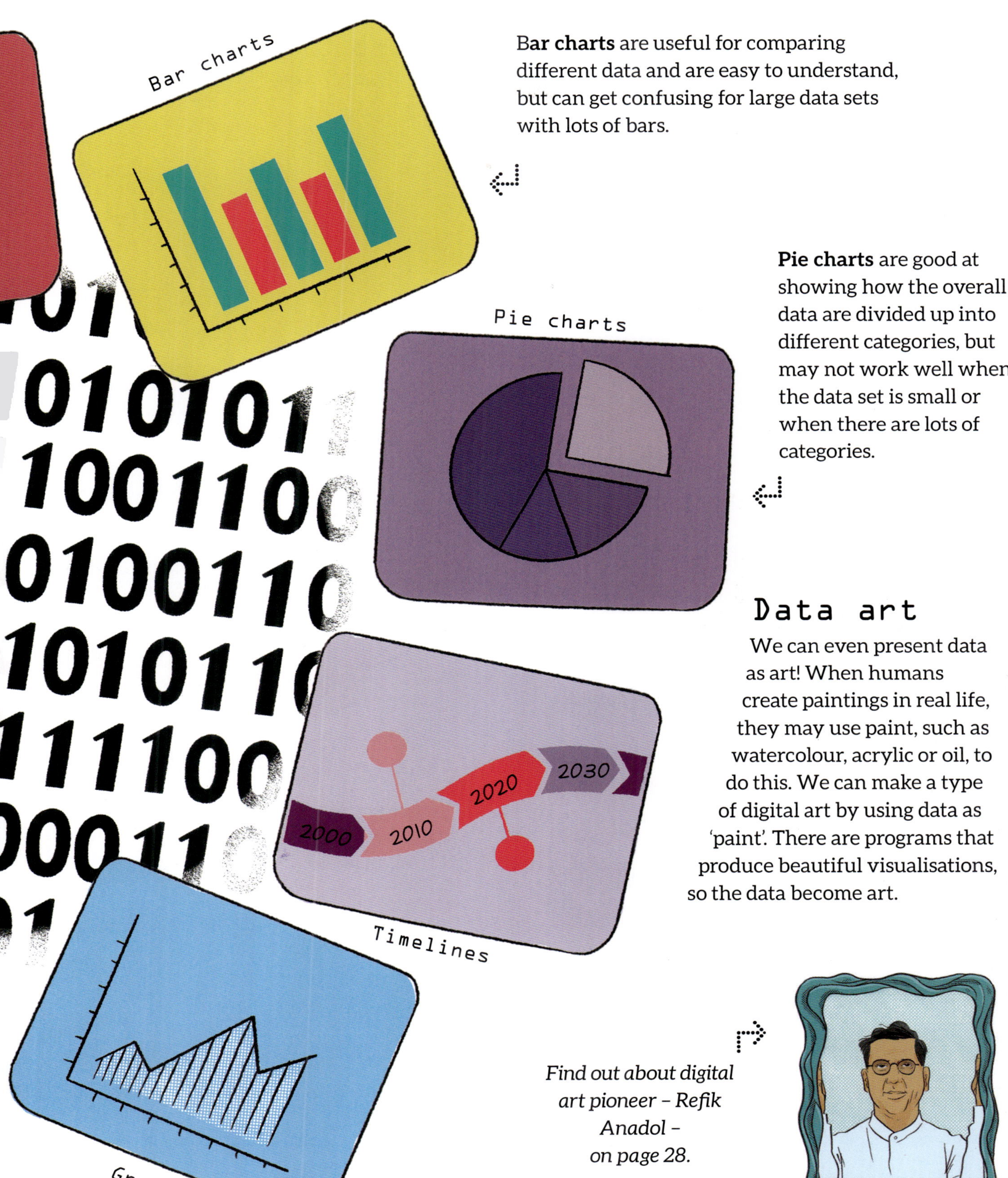

Bar charts are useful for comparing different data and are easy to understand, but can get confusing for large data sets with lots of bars.

Pie charts are good at showing how the overall data are divided up into different categories, but may not work well when the data set is small or when there are lots of categories.

Data art

We can even present data as art! When humans create paintings in real life, they may use paint, such as watercolour, acrylic or oil, to do this. We can make a type of digital art by using data as 'paint'. There are programs that produce beautiful visualisations, so the data become art.

Find out about digital art pioneer – Refik Anadol – on page 28.

Big data

When do data become **BIG?** When there are too
many pieces of data or they get too complicated
to be stored and processed by traditional
methods, then we have big data.

The four Vs

Big data are said to have four Vs:

1. There are huge amounts of data (**volume**).
2. They are produced very fast (**velocity**).
3. They can be of different types (**variety**).
4. They can be messy with mistakes (having low
   veracity, which is another word
   for truth or accuracy).

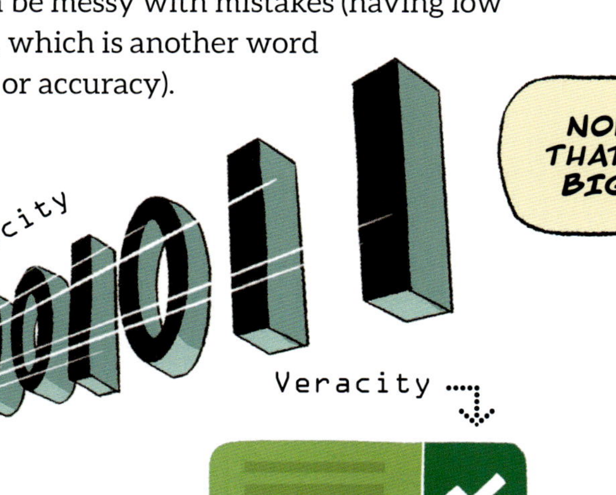

Examples of big data

Any collection of data with at least the
first three of the four Vs mentioned
above can be thought of as big data.

For example, over a long period of time:

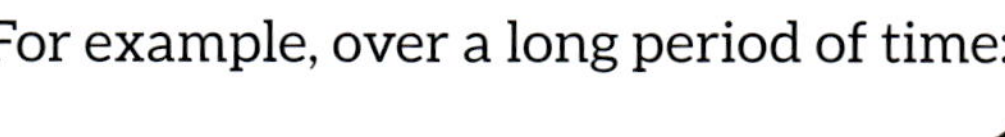
all the different medical data
of everyone in a country … 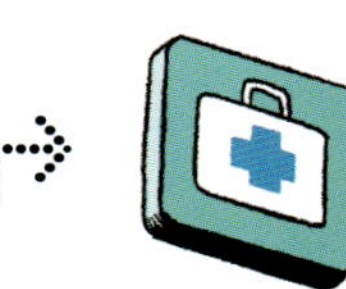

… data on weather conditions
recorded in different ways across the world … 

… or all the posts on a popular
social media platform, can
be thought of as big data. 

Big data = big challenges and big value

Big data are likely to grow very fast, be hugely varied in type and can have gaps, mistakes and unrelated content. All these factors make them hard to work with. Processing big data requires extra effort to confirm accuracy and fairness.

However, the content of big data can be very valuable to people and organisations. This makes some sorts of big data very tempting for hackers to try to see or steal. So big data need to have extra-robust security in place. (See pages 24–25 for more on security.)

Find out about information security pioneer – Dorothy Denning – on page 28.

Big uses of big data

Analysing big data and getting insights from them can help governments and companies make better decisions, work more efficiently and provide better services.

For example, when analysing lots of weather data from all over the world, meteorologists can find patterns or shifts in climate change more quickly.

Or by analysing transactions from a large sample of the population, banks can discover patterns that may reveal crimes, such as people trying to steal money.

Getting the most out of data

Usually, we collect data for a specific purpose and use them for that purpose. But with recent advances in computer science, we can get a lot more from these data. Here we look at two techniques that can give us new insights from data we already have.

Mining the data

Data mining is the process of finding useful information, such as patterns and insights, that are present in large amounts of data, even though the data may not have been collected for this purpose.

Underground mining

How it works

Just as mining underground pulls out valuable materials from the earth, data mining pulls out valuable information from data. For example, data mining has been used by astronomers to discover new objects and types of phenomena in space.

Data mining can make use of the second practice, **machine learning**, as part of the process.

Find out about data mining pioneer – Timnit Gebru – on page 29.

Machines learning from data

Machine learning is the process of a computer program discovering patterns based on existing data, so that it can make predictions about new data it has not seen before. Just as humans can learn from examples, machine learning programs attempt to learn from existing data.

Using our example of astronomy, machine learning can be used to classify newly discovered objects in space. This learning is based on what we already know about the characteristics of different space objects.

The rights and wrongs

Using techniques such as data mining and machine learning allows people and organisations to make new discoveries in fields such as astronomy, medicine, sales and sport. However, there can be problems with this.

Machine learning programs require enormous amounts of good quality data to learn to make accurate predictions. But the **quality** and **source** of big data are hard to guarantee.

For example, the data may have been collected from people who were not told (or who do not understand) how their data might be used. This can result in private information being made available to others without permission, or poor and irrelevant data being used by accident.

Keeping data secure

Some of the data we collect and store can be very personal or valuable. It is important to make sure that these data are available only to those who should have access to them.

Data security concerns

Data security attempts to keep data safe from harm. Computer scientists must think about the security of everything related to the secure use and storage of data, including:

How it's done

Let's look at some data security methods that take these concerns into account.

Physical security is the process of keeping data safe from disasters, such as fires and floods, and from thieves. Locks, security cameras, alarms and fire safety measures can help with this.

Encryption is the process of using an algorithm to change normal data (called plaintext) into a form that does not make sense (called ciphertext). People who are allowed to see the data will be able to change the altered data back to the original form and read them.

Access control is the process of making sure that only people who absolutely need the data for their work have access to them. Each person can see only the minimum amount of data necessary.

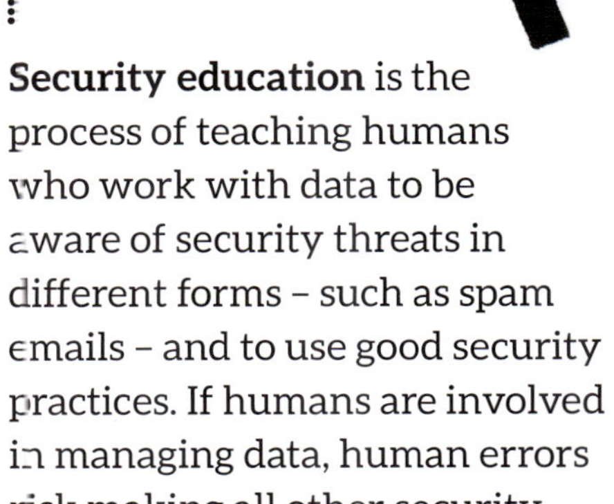

Security education is the process of teaching humans who work with data to be aware of security threats in different forms – such as spam emails – and to use good security practices. If humans are involved in managing data, human errors risk making all other security measures useless!

Backup is the process of regularly making copies of important data so that if the original data are lost or damaged, we still have copies of them.

A trip into the future of data ...

Scientists, governments and businesses have been making more and more use of more and more data in the last twenty years. What can we expect from data in the future?

Data from everywhere, all the time

In the near future, data collection is likely to become even more widespread than it is today. Human and machine activities and our environments will be monitored and analysed, unless we 'opt out' – this means we have to **ask not** to be included instead of asking to be included.

It's all automated

Data collection, storage, analysis and reporting will be done automatically by computers without humans needing to do the work.

Everyone is a data scientist

We will be surrounded by huge amounts of data about every aspect of our lives, so most people will learn to understand data more, and use them to make decisions with the help of computers.

What then for AI?

AI is the ability of computer programs to copy the way humans make decisions and solve problems. As more advances are made in AI, it can help humans better manage and understand large amounts of data, with increasing accuracy. AI can also automate more data-related tasks that are currently done by humans.

A data-driven future for all

Having access to lots of useful data can help us make better decisions for us, our families, our communities, our work and our planet. At the same time, we will become more aware of the need to keep our personal data private and safe, and to think carefully about the impact of our data use on the planet and its resources.

Pioneer portraits

Refik Anadol (1985–)

… is a Turkish–American media artist and pioneer in art that is produced by machine intelligence. He creates digital paintings and sculptures driven by data and machine learning. His work has been displayed in many parts of the world including Asia, Australia, Europe and America.

Edgar F. Codd (1923–2003)

… was a British computer scientist well known for his contributions in the area of databases. He invented the relational model, which is a logical and still widely used way of structuring databases. (Data in a relational model are organised in tables that show the relationships both between individual datum and groups of data.)

Sergey Brin (1973–) and Larry Page (1973–)

… are the two Americans who co-founded Google, which is one of the largest technology companies in the world. Google has released important products in the areas of Internet search engines, cloud computing, AI, online advertising, electronic devices, and software for end users. Because of the popularity of Google's search engine, 'google' is now used as a verb to mean 'do an Internet search' to find information online.

Dorothy Denning (1945–)

… is an American computer scientist famous for her work on information security. She particularly contributed to advances in intrusion detection (watching out for suspicious or unwanted activity on computer networks) and encryption (see page 25).

Timnit Gebru (1983-)

… is an Eritrean–Ethiopian computer scientist, who works on algorithmic bias (making algorithms fairer) and data mining. She highlights the need to use data and algorithms in a way that is fair to all. (An algorithm is a set of instructions or steps to be followed in solving a problem or completing a task.)

Fei-Fei Li (1976-)

… is a Chinese–American computer scientist, who is well known for her work on artificial intelligence. She is the inventor of ImageNet, a large data set containing millions of images, which has been very important for advances in the AI areas of machine learning and computer vision.

Claude Shannon (1916-2001)

… was an American mathematician and computer scientist, who is known as the 'father of information theory'. He is well-known for his work on ways to encode (convert to a specific format) and send information between two points (computers or other devices). He also introduced the idea of a bit (short for binary digit – 0 or 1) as a basic unit of information.

Ben Shneiderman (1947-)

… is an American computer scientist, who has made many contributions to the fields of human–computer interaction and information visualisation. He has proposed new visualisations, such as treemaps and lifelines, and developed the Information Visualisation Mantra ('Overview first, zoom and filter, then details-on-demand'). The Mantra is widely used to show data in user-friendly ways.

Karen Spärck Jones (1935–2007)

... was a Norwegian–British computer scientist well known for her work on information retrieval, which is the process of finding and getting (retrieving) data that are relevant for a particular task. Her work forms the basis of online search engines that we use all the time.

John Tukey (1915–2000)

.... was a statistician, who is thought of as one of the fathers of data science. He came up with the term 'data analysis'. He pioneered the idea of exploring data to find new knowledge (called exploratory data analysis), instead of simply using them to confirm or reject hypotheses (called confirmatory data analysis).

Further information

Books to read:

Why AI? by Dr Dharini Balasubramaniam (Wayland, 2024)
For a deeper dive into the details and debates around artificial intelligence

Super Tech (series) by Clive Gifford (Wayland, 2024)
For information about technology in space, gross tech, robots, AI and even dinosaurs!

Websites to visit:

datasciencecampus.ons.gov.uk/capability/bitesize-data-science-for-kids/ age-banded workshops for children to learn how to work with data

https://dataschools.education/data-education-resources/ resources for teachers with lots of 'plugged' and 'unplugged' data activities for pupils

Places to visit:

**The National Museum of Computing
www.tnmoc.org/**

**Science Museum
www.sciencemuseum.org.uk**

**Centre for Computing History
www.computinghistory.org.uk**

**Science and Industry Museum
www.scienceandindustrymuseum.org.uk**

https://teachcomputing.org/blog/data-science-and-data-skills-in-the-primary-school-classroom aimed at teachers, this blog covers the importance of data literacy in primary school children

https://www.tableau.com/blog/3-activities-help-kids-introduce-joy-data-45386 fun, age-banded data activities for kids.

Glossary

algorithm a set of instructions or steps to be followed in solving a problem or completing a task

arithmetic a branch of mathematics that deals with what we can do with numbers, such as addition and subtraction

artificial intelligence (AI) computer programs that imitate how humans make decisions and solve problems

astronomer a scientist who studies space and objects in space, such as stars and planets

automation the use of machines to complete tasks, with little or no human involvement

census the process of collecting and recording data about everyone in an area, such as a country

classification the process of grouping data that share common features into categories

climate change long-term changes in weather patterns

cloud a computing service, usually offering software and data storage, that can be accessed over a network

composite something made up of a number of parts

computer science the study of, or information related to, computations and how far computations can be automated

computer scientist someone who has studied computer science and works in this area

computer security the process of protecting computers and the data stored in them from theft

computer vision a field of AI that allows computer programs to understand digital images and videos

data details we collect and store about things that help with completing tasks or solving problems

data analysis the process of discovering useful information from data for making decisions or solving problems

data mining the process of finding useful information that is present in large amounts of data, even though the data may not have been collected for this purpose

data set a collection of data that can be used for various purposes, such as finding information or training programs

device a machine produced for a specific purpose

encryption the process of changing data into a form that can't be understood so that only those who have permission can change them back to the original form

end user a person using a computer-based solution

hacker someone who tries to access computer systems or data without permission to do so

hardware physical parts of a computer or device

human-computer interaction (HCI) a field in computer science that studies the different ways people interact with computers

information meaning that is obtained from the interpretation of data

intelligence the ability to gain knowledge and skills, and to use them in a logical and sensible way

Internet a worldwide network of networks, connecting huge numbers of computers and devices

knowledge the understanding of a subject or topic

machine learning a field of AI that uses data and algorithms to learn to make decisions, as humans might learn from examples

meteorologist a scientist who studies weather and more generally what happens in Earth's atmosphere

network a collection of connected computers or devices that can exchange data with one another

online being available via a computer network

phenomenon (plural phenomena) an interesting event that can be observed

pioneer one of the first people to do something

predict state that something will happen in the future

program a set of instructions written for a computer to carry out

reporting the process of presenting data in an easy-to-understand form

robust strong; not likely to fail

search engine software that helps users find information and websites online

software a set of programs used for a specific purpose, such as operating a computer or completing a task

software engineering an organised way to create software, following good principles and practices

spam unwanted email

statistics the mathematical study of how data can be collected, interpreted, explained and presented

summarising explaining the meaning of something in a shorter and often simpler way

technology the result of applying science to practical problems to produce solutions

transaction an exchange or transfer of money or goods

tree (in picturing data) a way of showing the different levels (hierarchy) and connections in data in the form of a tree

visualisation the process of creating images or diagrams to represent information so that it is easier to understand

Quiz yourself!

1. From bottom to top, which is the correct order of the words in the 'Wisdom' pyramid structure?
a) Knowledge -> Data -> Wisdom -> Information
b) Data -> Knowledge -> Information -> Wisdom
c) Data -> Information -> Knowledge -> Wisdom
d) Wisdom -> Information -> Knowledge -> Data

2. Where can we store data?
a) Computers
b) External hard drives
c) The cloud
d) All of the above

3. Which of the following is not a property of big data?
a) Large amounts of data
b) Data that are produced by big companies
c) Many different types of data
d) Data that are produced quickly

4. You have to record the colour of a dog's fur for a data-gathering activity. Which of these is a valid answer?
a) Brown
b) Purple
c) Green
d) Pink

5. How can encryption help to keep data secure?
a) It backs up data so we have copies if the original is lost
b) It limits the access people have to important data
c) It changes the form of the data, so that only people who are allowed access can change them back to the original form
d) All of the above

The answers are at the bottom of the page.

Index

Quiz answers: 1. c; 2. d; 3. b; 4. a; 5. c